At The CROSS

With The People Who Were There

Nelson Searcy &
C.A. Meyer

At the Cross: With the People Who Were There

Copyright © 2021 by Nelson Searcy

Published by Church Leader Insights U.S.A.

Printed in the United States of America

All rights reserved. No part of this publication may be reproduced, stored in a retrieval system, or transmitted in any form or by any means—for example, electronic, photocopy, or recording—without the prior written permission of the publisher. The only exception is brief quotations in printed reviews.

ISBN: 978-1-7363541-0-0

All Scripture quotations, unless otherwise indicated, are taken from the Holy Bible, New Living Translation, copyright © 1996, 2004, 2007, 2013, 2015 by Tyndale House Foundation. Used by permission of Tyndale House Publishers, Inc., Carol Stream, Illinois 60188. All rights reserved.

CONTENTS

Introduction 7

1. At the Cross
   with the Hardened Skeptic 13

2. At the Cross
   with the Devoted Servant 31

3. At the Cross
   with the Heartbroken Mother 51

4. At the Cross
   with the Condemned Criminal 71

You, at the Cross 85

Acknowledgments 89

To everyone Jesus loved and died for at the cross nearly 2,000 years ago.

†

INTRODUCTION

The lights dimmed in the auditorium. The cross's shadow laid starkly across the stage. All over the wood were sticky notes written with the prayers of the congregants: tiny, neat, and large, oblong letters on upturning yellow squares. They made a checkerboard of the oak beams, paper-thin but weighted with anticipation, joy, regret, and secret suffering.

The pastor told his church to write down on the provided sticky notes all the burdens in their wearied hearts, all the answered miracles worthy of praise—anything they needed to give to God—and then "lay them at the cross."

At the cross.

You may have heard that phrase before. You may have heard it so many times it's become a catchphrase in your mind. Amid all the distractions we face today it's easy to forget the true origin story of believers' salvation and why it's so important.

Even if you know the story of the Crucifixion and Resurrection, that the Son of God died for your sins and was raised again on the third day, conquering sin and death, stop for a moment and ask yourself: what might it have been like to be truly at the cross?

What happened there nearly 2,000 years ago?

Who was there to see it?

What can I discover through their experiences?

In this book, we're going to explore the events that took place that Friday afternoon when obeying His Father's will, Jesus Christ was nailed to a cross for us. We're going to gaze up at those blood-stained wooden beams through the eyes of four witnesses: a hardened skeptic, a devoted servant, a heartbroken mother, and a condemned criminal.

But you're going to see yourself among

these pages, too.

No matter what your story is, you'll likely recognize something in each of these characters, people Scripture tells us were there the day Jesus paid the ultimate sacrifice on behalf of the world. In their struggle, ignorance, pain, frustration, heartbreak, and healing, we see the beauty of God's grace and mercy playing out. We see the power of what Jesus did at the cross and how it is still just as powerful, just as life-changing, just as soul-saving as ever.

You may think there's nothing new to learn about Jesus' experience, or that you've read enough books about the events we call Easter. But for those moments in your life in which the lights grow dim, in which your burdens weigh heavily on your heart, and you're called to surrender them at the cross, you'll want to know what "at the cross" looks like. When what you struggle with is more than what a sticky note can bear, you'll desire for those words—*at the cross*—to be more than a catchphrase. Because they are. Look to the apostle Paul.

In a letter to the Galatians, he wrote, "As for me, may I never boast about anything except the cross of our Lord Jesus Christ. Because of that cross, my interest in this world has been crucified, and the world's interest in me has also died." (Galatians 6:14)

You see, at the cross is where our sins are forgiven.

At the cross is where our brokenness is healed.

At the cross is where our hope is secured, in Jesus, forever.

Let's go there...

INTRODUCTION

"Alas, and Did My Savior Bleed"
A Church Hymn by Isaac Watts (1707)

The title of the book you hold in your hands is based on one of the most famous Easter church hymns of all time ("hymn" being just a fancy name for songs sung at church). Throughout this book, we've offered selections from this powerful work to inspire you and reinforce the teachings of this book. We encourage you to take a moment to reflect on these lyrics; even though the 18th Century language may not be common today, it will allow you to experience a different perspective of what being "At the Cross" means. Turn the page for the first selection...

AT THE CROSS

Alas, and did my Savior bleed,
And did my Sovereign die!
Would He devote that sacred head
For such a worm as I?

At the cross, at the cross where
I first saw the light,
And the burden of my heart rolled away,
It was there by faith I received my sight,
And now I am happy all the day!

"Alas, and Did My Savior Bleed"
Isaac Watts, *Hymns and Spiritual Songs* (1707)

1

AT THE CROSS WITH THE HARDENED SKEPTIC

*"Jesus said, 'Father, forgive them,
for they don't know what they are doing.'"*
Luke 23:34

Under the stark rays of a late morning sun, on a skull-shaped hill named Golgotha outside ancient Jerusalem, the Son of God allowed Himself to be hung from a wooden cross.

Whipped, mocked, spit upon, and betrayed, Jesus endured the worst of injustices at the hands of His enemies. Though He lived a life entirely free of sin, Jesus took on the criminal punishment of death on a cross abandoned by His closest friends, condemned by the religious leaders of His community, and delivered over to this terrible end by the Roman government.

His body was already weak and torn and sleep deprived. A thorny crown pressed into the skin of His head, cruelly twisted together by Roman soldiers. These same soldiers had flogged Him with a lead-tipped whip, tearing the flesh off His body to ensure He would die faster on the cross. They had mocked Him by dressing Him up as a pretend king, saying, "Hail, King of the Jews!" They had beaten Him and spat on Him before nailing Him to a final humiliation in the middle of two robbers on crosses to His right and left. Jesus' response was incredible.

Luke 23:34 tells us: "Jesus said, 'Father, forgive them, for they don't know what they are doing.' And the soldiers gambled for his clothes by throwing dice."

Clearly, for the Roman soldier keeping guard below Jesus on the cross, gambling for His clothing, this was a typical day on the job—yet another crucifixion.

Reserved for the lowest of the low,

crucifixion wasn't just meant to kill the criminal, but to humiliate him. It was to send a powerful message to all those who saw the cross that Rome was in control. When Roman soldiers crucified someone, it wasn't the spikes going through the criminal's wrists and feet that killed him. Death would come when he was eventually so weak he couldn't lift his head, leading him to suffocate. It was a shaming death and extraordinarily painful.

The very symbol of the cross became an instrument the Romans used to terrorize people. It said, "We are superior. You are inferior." Even a Roman statesman, the famous Marcus Tullius Cicero, called crucifixion the cruelest and most undignified punishment. He urged Roman citizens to turn their thoughts, eyes, and ears away from even the thought of the cross. But for the Roman soldier who helped crucify Jesus, it was all in a day's work. Mocking, beating, torturing, and killing rebels was common practice. It's easy to imagine how a soldier could be a hardened skeptic on the morning he oversaw Jesus' execution.

Luke 23:35-38 shows us as much: "The crowd watched and the leaders scoffed. 'He saved others,' they said, 'let him save himself if he is really God's Messiah, the Chosen One.' The soldiers mocked him, too, by offering him a drink of sour wine. They called out to him, 'If you are the King of the Jews, save yourself!' A sign was fastened above him with these words: 'This is the King of the Jews.'"

Little did the Roman soldier know, Jesus was not just another rebel to the Roman Empire and its overseer, Tiberius Caesar. This crucifixion would not be like any other. It would be a moment that changed him, and the world, forever. Even though the Roman soldier woke up that morning an unbeliever—in all likelihood, a hard-hearted skeptic—by that afternoon, his life, and his heart, would be transformed by God's grace.

Luke 23:44-46 continues: "By this time

it was about noon, and darkness fell across the whole land until three o'clock. The light from the sun was gone. And suddenly, the curtain in the sanctuary of the Temple was torn down the middle. Then Jesus shouted, 'Father, I entrust my spirit into your hands!' And with those words he breathed his last."

The events leading up to the moment of Jesus' death happened very quickly. He had only been arrested the night before. But by 9 a.m. the next morning, Jesus had been put on trial, brought before Pontius Pilate, the Roman governor, and sentenced to death. Most people condemned to death by crucifixion survived for several hours, some even clinging to life for days. But Jesus was tortured so brutally He died faster than most would, suffocating after about six hours on the cross and dying around 3 p.m. that day.

When Jesus died, several extraordinary things occurred. The Bible tells us there was an earthquake. During the quake, rocks split apart, and in the temple, the Jews' holy place of worship, a curtain separating the area where everyday people could go and the sacred place where only the priests could enter split in two. No longer did sin and its consequences keep the people from drawing near to their God.

On the cross, Jesus took on the punishment for every person's sin. That punishment is death. Even someone like the Roman soldier was then able to go directly to God and have a personal relationship with Him. The same is true for us today.

But God wasn't finished doing miracles that afternoon. The Bible reveals not only was the temple curtain split in two, but tombs in and around Jerusalem were opened. Godly men and women were raised from the dead. And the Roman soldier witnessed this.

Matthew 27:54 reveals, in a moment, his cynicism melted away. Miraculously, he believed: "The Roman officer and the other soldiers at the crucifixion were terrified by the earthquake and all that had happened. They said, 'This man truly was the Son of God!'"

At this moment, our hardened skeptic, the Roman soldier at the foot of the cross, was saved by God's grace—a gift of love and mercy that isn't earned but is given by God simply because He desires to give it.

Romans 6:23 says it best: "For the wages of sin is death, but the free gift of God is eternal life through Christ Jesus our Lord."

It was by God's grace, through faith in Jesus, that the soldier was rescued from his sin.

We can learn a thing or two from his story. Grace is God's undeserved favor, forgiveness and kindness on sinners, so let's explore some Grace Lessons from 2,000 years ago that still apply today.

†

Grace Lesson #1:
God Is Always At Work
Drawing People To Him.

The life of a Roman soldier in the first century wasn't easy. It was a lot like the lives of those in the military today.

Called to be far from home, far from their families, they lived in difficult circumstances and worked in hostile territories. Covered in weighty armor and weaponry, they would often start their day before dawn, packing their tents and kits loaded with heavy rations and tools. Marching up to 20 miles a day, they were at the whim of the Roman government, whether that meant putting down rebellions, building walls, forts, and roads, or crucifying rebels. You can imagine when our Roman soldier woke up that Friday morning, he was expecting another day of the same old drudgery.

Maybe your life looks similar: the alarm clock goes off, and you eat the same thing for breakfast. You take the same route to work. When you get to work, you do the same task over and over and over again. It seems futile. You wonder to yourself, "What's the purpose? What's the value, the *eternal* value in what I'm doing?" That futility can harden you to the point where you don't recognize God when He's working in your life. You may start to doubt He cares or that He has a purpose and plan for you.

The Roman soldier wasn't aware when he woke up that Friday morning that he was about to encounter God's radical grace. He didn't see it, but God was about to cut through the mundane of his life, the sin in his heart, and change him forever. That's how powerful God's love is.

Romans 2:4 says, "Don't you see how wonderfully kind, tolerant, and patient God is with you? Does this mean nothing to you? Can't you see that his kindness is intended to turn you from your sin?"

The way God drew the Roman soldier to

Him, at the foot of the same cross to which that soldier had just nailed His son, should give you a greater perspective on God's character and ways. Through the good and bad in your life, even when you don't recognize it, He's working for your very best. God wants you to trust Him with your purpose, with your future, with everything. His intent is to turn you away from sin by His grace—that gift of love and mercy. Is it any wonder He's described as a good Father?

Grace Lesson #2: God Demonstrates His Grace At The Cross.

Try to imagine the number of people the Roman soldier mocked and tortured and killed—how overwhelmingly this behavior was a part of his identity. It must've hardened him.

On the morning he nailed Jesus to the cross, it's obvious he had no idea who he was executing. Worse, he probably didn't care. It was one more person, one more rebel, to mock, torture, and crucify. If God were selfish, vengeful, and fickle like one of us humans, the Roman soldier who killed His Son would be the last person He would want to save.

But God is not like us. He's holy. He's perfect. He has this incredible, perfect, faithful love for sinners, sinners like us, sinners like this Roman soldier.

And Luke 23:34 tells us Jesus Himself, while dying, prayed for God to show mercy to His enemies.

This is the scandal of Christianity. This is the scandal of God's grace.

Despite the suffering the world inflicted on Him, Jesus willingly gave Himself on the cross so everyone who believed in Him would be saved, even the Roman soldier who crucified Him.

Think about that for a moment.

Maybe you would've done the same for

the people you love the most—your parents or your spouse, or your closest friend. Maybe, if they'd done something that bore a cost, for their slate to be wiped clean, you would take death for them. Perhaps you would even be crucified for them on a cross, for the people you love and who love you. That would be an unbelievably noble thing to do.

But would you get up there for your enemies? For people who hate you, for people who defiantly sin or for people you don't even know? Would you be as willing to wipe their slates clean if it cost you your life?

Romans 5:7-8 says, "Now, most people would not be willing to die for an upright person, though someone might perhaps be willing to die for a person who is especially good. But God showed his great love for us by sending Christ to die for us while we were still sinners."

This is what real love looks like: being willing to die for someone who doesn't love you, for someone who doesn't even deserve it. And that's what Jesus did. That's what the Bible calls "grace." Grace is God's love, showered on us, even though we don't deserve it.

Grace Lesson #3: God Uses You To Share His Transforming Grace.

The apostle Matthew doesn't reveal to us what happened to the Roman soldier after Jesus died on the cross that day. We don't know where he went or who he talked to, or in what ways his encounter with the cross changed his life.

Maybe he stayed on that skull-shaped hill called Golgotha, gazing up at the sky and the blood-soaked cross, undone by the prayer Jesus prayed for him. Perhaps he stumbled home in a daze, telling everyone he came across of the grace Jesus showed him despite his sins. We can't know for sure. What we do know is once you encounter the power of the cross and believe in your heart who Jesus is and what He did, it changes you. When you experience God's grace, it transforms your heart. And God uses that transformation to draw others to Himself.

Only the power of God's grace can break through a darkened heart. The Roman soldier was instantly transformed when he declared his belief in Jesus, saying, "This man truly was the Son of God!"

The same is true for you. If you openly declare Jesus is Lord and believe in your heart God raised Him from the dead after His crucifixion, you will be saved, too. In an instant, you can experience God's grace and salvation.

The author of the book of Hebrews teaches how we can follow Jesus, even during difficult times, by reminding us of His sacrifice.

He writes in Hebrews 12:2, "We do this by keeping our eyes on Jesus, the champion who initiates and perfects our faith. Because of the joy awaiting him, he endured the cross, disregarding its shame. Now he is seated in the place of honor beside God's throne."

†

Although the Crucifixion took place nearly 2,000 years ago, believers and non-believers around the world today recognize it as the moment in time that changed all of human history. Jesus Christ, the sinless Son of God, willingly endured the cross to the point of death, and through His death, a weapon of shame was transformed into the ultimate symbol of hope for the world. Although Jesus died on that cross, He was resurrected three days later, and that changes everything.

His resurrection is the cornerstone of the Christian faith: Jesus is alive. Sin and death are defeated. When we believe in Jesus, we can have our relationship with God restored. We can be reshaped into the people God created us to be. We can have a home in heaven. There is no other moment in human history that offers more hope, more grace.

That's why it's so important to look closer at the cross. When you understand the death and shame of it, the fact each of us, as sinners, deserved an end like that, yet Jesus took it for us—only then can you truly understand the power of the resurrection, the beauty of God's love, and the radical, transforming grace God gives to each of us who believe in His Son.

Was it for sins that I had done,
He groaned upon the tree?
Amazing pity! Grace unknown!
And love beyond degree!

At the cross, at the cross where
I first saw the light,
And the burden of my heart rolled away,
It was there by faith I received my sight,
And now I am happy all the day!

"Alas, and Did My Savior Bleed"
Isaac Watts, *Hymns and Spiritual Songs* (1707)

2

AT THE CROSS WITH THE DEVOTED SERVANT

"Standing near the cross were Jesus' mother, and his mother's sister, Mary (the wife of Clopas), and Mary Magdalene."
John 19:25

We don't know everyone who was there at the cross with Jesus the day He died for our sins. But Scripture tells us while most of His disciples ran away, too afraid to go all the way to the cross with their Savior, a few specific women were courageous enough, faithful enough, to remain at His side.

John 19:25 says, "Standing near the cross were Jesus' mother and His mother's sister, Mary, the wife of Clopas and Mary Magdalene."

The last Mary mentioned in this verse, Mary Magdalene, is a figure who is often misunderstood. It's through her eyes, as a devoted servant of Jesus, that we can look at that day on the cross with a new perspective.

Throughout history and popular fiction, Mary Magdalene has been the subject of rumors, conspiracy theories, and flat-out myths—and this was true long before social media. In many Christians' minds, she's thought of to be a woman with a bad reputation. But who was she? Where did this woman, one of the three women named Mary at the foot of Jesus' cross, come from? Why was she there that day? Who was Jesus to her, and she to Him?

The truth is, we don't know everything we'd like to know about Mary Magdalene's background, as she's only mentioned a handful of times in the New Testament. But considering she's there at the moment of Jesus' crucifixion, clearly devoted to Him in His life, death, and resurrection three days later, it's important to debunk some of the myths surrounding her and her past.

†

Myth #1:
Magdalene Was Mary's Last Name.

Mary's second name was not her last name. It points to the place she was from—the city of Magdala, a thriving town on the Sea of Galilee three miles north of Tiberius. Magdala was known for textile manufacturing and fine dyes, a city of trade and wealth.

The name of someone's hometown in place of what we would call in our modern era someone's last name was common in Jesus' time. In fact, throughout the Bible, Jesus is often referred to as Jesus the Nazarene since He grew up in Nazareth.

Myth #2:
Jesus And Mary Magdalene Had A Romantic Relationship.

The idea Mary Magdalene was romantically linked to Jesus is an age-old myth unfortunately helped along today by the 2003 novel *Da Vinci Code* by Dan Brown. There is no biblical or historical evidence Mary Magdalene was anything other than a faithful follower and supporter of Jesus.

Myth #3:
Mary Magdalene Was A Prostitute.

Pope Gregory I, bishop of Rome in the late sixth and early seventh centuries, was the first to associate Mary Magdalene with the unnamed repentant prostitute written of in Luke 7:37-50. Many classical paintings of Mary Magdalene portray her in this light, despite the lack of biblical or historical evidence it's a truthful depiction.

†

What is most certainly not a myth about Mary Magdalene was that she was fiercely devoted to Jesus and unwavering in her commitment to Him as her Savior. She was so committed to Him that even when Jesus' closest disciples abandoned Him at His moment of greatest suffering, she was there.

For followers of Jesus, Mary Magdalene is an important figure to look at because we find a life of profound devotion to Jesus in her.

In a world filled with distractions, it's easy to fall away from God's plan for us or to lose our passion for His word. In a society often driven by social media, it's easy to become so self-absorbed we lose our connection to Jesus and seek meaning in someone or something other than God. But when we do that, life begins to feel futile and frustrating. We become burdened by our sin again, forgetting the power of the cross and the beauty of a life devoted to God.

But what does it look like to be entirely devoted to Jesus? What decisions should we make so we can better follow Him in every circumstance?

Decision #1:
Allow God To Restore Your Broken Life.

Mary's journey with Jesus began long before that day on the cross. Like many of us, before she met Jesus and became His devoted follower, Mary had a broken life.

We pick up her story in Luke 8:1-2, which captures a time near the beginning of Jesus' ministry as He's teaching, traveling, and healing people in need.

Scripture says, "Soon afterward Jesus began a tour of the nearby towns and villages preaching and announcing the Good News about God's kingdom. He took His twelve disciples with Him along with some women who had been cured of evil spirits and diseases. Among them were Mary Magdalene from whom He had cast out seven demons."

Someone possessed by demons would've been considered an outcast by society in Jesus' day. Their community would've treated them as impure, a stigma they carried around with them everywhere they went. It's hard to picture someone possessed by demons from our modern perspective, let alone seven of them. But we know that throughout the Bible, the number seven is used to portray completeness. So, as seven demons possessed Mary, it may be this number was used to show how completely broken and messed-up her life was. And it's in this impure, broken, utterly messed-up state that Mary first met Jesus.

The Bible doesn't tell us exactly what happened from there. But at some point in Mary's interaction with Jesus, He healed her. He set her free of her demons. He restored her, and she decided to follow Him, even to the cross.

Maybe there's a part of your life right now that feels broken. Perhaps you're at a job that makes you miserable, and you can't see a way out of it. Maybe you'd always hoped you'd be married at this point in your life, but it hasn't played out that way. Maybe your finances put a crippling strain on your ability to enjoy life. Out of all of these broken dreams, you don't believe God could bring about something good.

You're not alone. The Bible tells us that while we're all created in the divine image of God, sin's existence in each of us has broken that image. And in all our shattered pieces, we don't resemble who God created us to be. Even the people in your life who you think are perfect—even they are broken by sin. Our sin separates us from God.

As a result, we're hurting. We're empty. We're lost. We're confused. We're angry. We feel brokenness deeply in our life every day.

But when we look at Mary Magdalene, we see that God specializes in restoring broken people. When we look closer at her story, we learn that no matter how broken we feel, how completely shattered our lives seem to be, Jesus can heal and restore our broken lives when we believe and trust in Him.

Decision #2:
Use Your Gifts To Serve Others.

After Jesus restored her, Mary showed her devotion to Him by using her gifts to serve Him and others. We see throughout the Gospels that Mary went from a woman defined by brokenness to a woman who devoted her life to serving Jesus and His mission. Whether it was providing food for Him and His disciples or securing for them a place to stay throughout their ministry, Mary served Jesus in any way she could. She may have been one of the people Jesus sent out to spread his message from town to town (Luke 10:1-23).

She didn't have to do any of these things—Jesus healed and saved her as a gift—but she did them out of gratitude. After Jesus healed her and removed her demon-possessed stigma, she could've responded to Him by saying, "Thank you, Jesus. I appreciate it. But I'm going to keep living life the way I used to."

Many of us might've responded to God that way. Instead, Mary decided to use her gifts, time, and resources to serve her Savior and to bless others. Not because she had to, but because she wanted to.

When we encounter Jesus, and He begins to heal our brokenness, we face the same choice. We can use our restored lives to live for ourselves, or we can surrender them to serve God and the people He places around us to love.

But, you see, the gifts and talents we each possess are gifts and talents God gave us. And He didn't give them to us to keep hidden or use for ourselves. He gave them to us for His purposes, to serve His mission and His people. Still, the choice on whether or not we use these gifts is up to us.

We know this from 1 Peter 4:10, which says, "God has given each of you a gift from His great variety of spiritual gifts. Use them well to serve one another."

Decision #3:
Give Generously To God's Mission.

Referencing a group of Jesus' supporters, Luke 8:2-3 says, "Among them were Mary Magdalene, from whom He had cast out seven demons; Joanna, the wife of Chuza, Herod's business manager; Susanna and many others who were contributing from their own resources to support Jesus and His disciples."

Here, we read not only did Mary use her gifts to serve Jesus, but she also used her money and resources to help fund God's mission. And this wasn't a one-time donation, either. For a period of approximately three years, Jesus and His disciples traveled around Israel, from town to town, ministering to people. During their travels, they had to eat. They had to have a place to stay. They needed supplies.

Mary's and others' generosity made Jesus' teaching and ministry possible.

Like Mary, how we invest our money will reflect if our lives are genuinely devoted to God and His mission. In other words, our lives will model generosity if we're entirely dedicated to God.

What we reap from choosing to be generous with the blessings God gives us is seeing our friends, family, coworkers, or neighbors changed by the Gospel of Jesus Christ.

We know about Mary's story today in part because of her generosity—the New Testament makes a point to note her devotion to Jesus by the giving of her resources. For Mary, this was money well spent.

Matthew 6:21 says, "Wherever your

treasure is, there the desires of your heart will also be."

Where Mary gave of her resources pointed directly to who she entrusted her heart to, and that's the case for us as well.

But even if you are entirely devoted to Jesus, and He heals your brokenness, and you're using your gifts and talents for Him, and you're being generous with what God has given you, it doesn't mean you're going to live a life devoid of problems. It doesn't mean you're not going to have heartache. Even after God has been active in your life and you're being faithful, there will be hard times. Just look at the cross: Jesus faced unbelievable cruelty and suffering, and He was the most faithful person ever to walk the earth.

If you want to read more about how to give generously to God's mission, check out The Generosity Secret *by Nelson Searcy.*

Decision #4:
Remain Faithful During Tough Times.

It's easy to be devoted when everything is going your way. But what about when life gets hard? Mary Magdalene remained loyal to Jesus even during the toughest of times, and the fact she was at the cross is significant, as it's mentioned in each of the Gospels: Matthew, Mark, Luke, and John.

Mark 15:40-41 says, "Some women were there, watching from a distance, including Mary Magdalene, Mary (the mother of James the younger and of Joseph), and Salome. They had been followers of Jesus and had cared for him while he was in Galilee…"

For many of Jesus' followers, at the point in which He was hanging on a cross, dying, all hope seemed lost. But we find Mary Magdalene even at this moment.

It wasn't safe that day to be in Jerusalem and be identified as a follower of Jesus. He was considered a radical. He had upset the religious and political system. So, anyone identified as being connected to Him in any way was in danger of arrest and execution themselves. Even Peter, Jesus' most outspoken disciple—the one who had promised Jesus he'd go all the way to the grave with Him just the night before—denied knowing who Jesus was three times.

But not Mary Magdalene. Seven demons had possessed her, she was an outcast in society, but Jesus didn't turn His back on her. Now, in His hour of need, Mary was going to stay faithful to Him, too.

We'll never have the honor Mary Magdalene had of literally following the Savior of the world to the cross, showing up for Him in the cruelest hours of His life as His devoted follower and friend. But what we can learn from her unwavering devotion to the Son of God is when we don't know what direction to take in life, when our courage is petering out, when it's growing increasingly risky to be an outspoken Christian, ==God is trustworthy and good and in control.==

Decision #5:
Keep Your Focus On Eternity.

As we've mentioned, the city of Magdala was known for textile manufacturing and dyes. While there's no evidence to confirm this, it could be Mary Magdalene was somehow connected with this industry. Scripture tells us she supported Jesus' ministry financially, and this connection with Magdala's textile and dyes could've allowed her to do so.

Experienced dye workers in Magdala would've known once a fabric is dyed, its original color is gone. Once they took a white cloth and colored it a darker shade, it would never be white again. It would be stained forever.

Some people view their lives that way.

Some of us see we've been stained by sin. We see how it's broken us, and we think we can never be who God wants us to be. We believe He can never use us or even love us because we're too stained and too broken.

But that's not true.

We know we are all created in God's image and that He meant for us to be pure and stainless and whole. But then sin entered the world, stained, and broke us. That sin now separates us from God. We see this tragedy and think there's nothing anyone can do about it. But the Bible tells us God saw our situation and stepped down from Heaven and came to earth. In all His perfection and wholeness, He entered a place filled with brokenness.

He did this by sending His Son, Jesus Christ, into a shattered world, where He lived a stainless life. Then, Jesus went to the cross and, at the cross, took upon Himself the sins of the entire world. Every sin you've ever committed, every sin you'll ever commit, Jesus took upon Himself when He allowed His body to be nailed to the cross. That sin went with Him to the grave. He was buried and stayed in the grave for three days, but then God raised Him from the dead, and so Jesus overcame the power of sin and death.

But the story is even greater than that.

Not only did Jesus overcome sin and death for the world, but the Bible tells us even as we stand in this state of sin, if we believe in Him, He will come into our lives and take what was stained and make it pure again.

That's what God does. He takes the broken pieces and puts them back together. He takes a stained life that couldn't possibly be made clean again and makes it clean, so we can stand before Him in all His holiness and perfection and become who He created us to be, accepted and loved by Him.

We will sin, again and again, every day of our lives. We are not perfect like God. But when we believe, sin does not have power over us. God's power overcame sin's power by what Jesus did at the cross.

AT THE CROSS WITH THE DEVOTED SERVANT

Well might the sun in darkness hide,
And shut His glories in,
When God, the mighty Maker, died
For man, His creature's sin.

At the cross, at the cross where
I first saw the light,
And the burden of my heart rolled away,
It was there by faith I received my sight,
And now I am happy all the day!

"Alas, and Did My Savior Bleed"
Isaac Watts, *Hymns and Spiritual Songs* (1707)

3

AT THE CROSS WITH THE HEARTBROKEN MOTHER

"When Jesus saw his mother standing there beside the disciple he loved, he said to her, 'Dear woman, here is your son.'"
John 19:26

Mary, the mother of Jesus, often strikes the hearts of believers differently. For some, when they remember Mary, a mental image of "Christmas Mary" comes to them, her cloaked head bowed as she sits in awe and quiet adoration, cradling the baby Jesus. Others recall "Crucifixion Mary," where Jesus' mother is crumpled over at the foot of the cross, agony stretching her face taut, eyes clouded with grief. Still, for others, it's "holy Mary" in a stained-glass window, her skin the hue of buttermilk, an angel's halo glistening over her head.

But there's more to Mary's story than Christmas and the Crucifixion. It's true she went from an apprehensive yet trusting teenager God chose to bear the Savior, to a mother in deep mourning having to watch Jesus die on a cross. It's true these two moments, and Mary's part in them, are what we remember most because of who is at their center—Jesus. But we also know from Scripture that Mary lived a lot of life between those events, and there's a lot we can learn from her.

And as for "holy Mary" in the stained-glass window, nowhere in the Bible are we told or led to believe Mary is someone we should pray to or consider holy. It's true the angel Gabriel called her favored by God, as Luke 1:28 records, and as the mother of the Messiah, Mary was chosen for an extraordinary task. But it's important to clarify she was not divine like God.

Mary was flawed, fear-filled at times, and burdened with genuine concerns any young mother in ancient Israel might have for herself and her family.

We know she and her carpenter husband Joseph, living in the Lower Galilee region of Israel, in a town called Nazareth, weren't wealthy. We know they had several children after Jesus. And we know at some point before Jesus began His public ministry at age 30, Joseph died. Then, as a widow and a single mother, Mary continued with her life's responsibilities.

When you gather all these details about her life—when the undeniably human, but remarkably obedient, Jewish woman from Nazareth emerges—it's plain God used Mary in much of the same way He uses us today—to bring about His good, pleasing, perfect will.

If we immerse ourselves in Mary's experience at Jesus' crucifixion, if we get on our knees in humbling, hopeful understanding of the sacrifice He made for us, we can discover what it truly means to be a follower of the Son of God. Because even in what had to have been the most challenging moment of her life as a mother, that Friday afternoon, those six hours, when Jesus hung on a cross, Mary stayed by His side as the obedient follower of God she was.

†

Discovery #1: Following Jesus Means Obeying Him.

Picture this: a young teenage girl is engaged to be married, and she finds out from an angel she's pregnant. Pregnant not from her fiancé, but by the Holy Spirit. Now, she's got to explain it to her parents. She's got to explain it to her fiancé, a man named Joseph. As scary and shaming as those conversations might be, it's even more frightening to think the people closest to her could stone her to death for conceiving a child outside of marriage.

Can you imagine being Mary at this moment? Can you think of how you would respond? Maybe you'd get angry with God, questioning the angel He sent to tell you of what was to come. Perhaps you'd be filled with fear over what your community would think of you, bearing a child revealed to you as the Son of God. Maybe, instead of seeing the indescribable blessing in it, you'd resent you were chosen for this task—mourning who you were before.

Luke 1:38 says, "Mary responded, 'I am the Lord's servant. May everything you have said about me come true.'"

Mary couldn't have known at that moment her selfless surrender to God was going to lead her to the foot of the cross. She had no clue that she'd watch her firstborn, Jesus Christ, the Son of God and Savior of the world, die the death that changed humanity.

She didn't know the suffering or the heartbreak that was to come. But even so, Mary trusted God. She listened to His voice above every other voice. She followed His will for her above any plans she'd dreamed up for herself. She didn't pick what parts of His Word to follow and what parts to ignore to avoid discomfort or pain or loss.

This is godly obedience.

Simply saying you're a Christian doesn't make you a follower of Jesus. There are plenty of people in the world who call themselves Christians, but when it comes to being obedient to God and following Jesus, they'd rather follow themselves. They'd rather be obedient to their own will. Even if you were born into a Christian family, go to church, read your Bible, and try to be a good person, those things don't make you a follower of Jesus.

Despite what you may have been taught, the primary way Jesus can tell if we love Him is not how often we go to church or how often we pray, but if we *obey* Him.

John 14:21 says, "Those who accept my commandments and obey them are the ones who love me…"

Obedience to God leads to God's best. Mary's obedience showed she loved Jesus enough to follow Him to the cross. It wasn't easy by any means, but it was God's best for her.

What does your obedience say about your love of Jesus? Everyone makes someone or something Lord of their life, whether it's money, fame, or another person. Ask yourself, if it's not Jesus, who or what has become Lord of your life? Where are you not being obedient to God?

You can trust Jesus enough to obey Him. Just look at the cross to see how much He loves you, to see the length and breadth and depth of that love.

Discovery #2:
Following Jesus Leads To Both Joy And Sorrow.

Forty days after His birth, Joseph and Mary took Jesus to the temple to be blessed, something every good Jewish family did. There, they met a godly man named Simeon. Simeon had waited his entire life to see the Messiah.

Luke 2:27-28 says, "So when Mary and Joseph came to present the baby Jesus to the Lord as the law required, Simeon was there. He took the child in his arms and praised God…"

Although many people may think only of Crucifixion Mary and the sorrow she felt to watch Jesus die on that cross, the Bible also shows moments of joy in Mary's experience, like this one with Simeon at the temple.

Luke 2:33-35 continues with the story:

"Jesus' parents were amazed at what was being said about him. Then Simeon blessed them, and he said to Mary, the baby's mother, 'This child is destined to cause many in Israel to fall, and many others to rise. He has been sent as a sign from God, but many will oppose him. As a result, the deepest thoughts of many hearts will be revealed..."

One can imagine the mixed emotions Mary must've felt at hearing what was to come in Jesus' future. The rise and the fall. The power and the opposition. The joy and the sorrow.

Then, at the end of Luke 2:35, Simeon speaks of Mary directly:

"...And a sword will pierce your very soul."

Mary must've known here that sorrow is as much a part of life as joy. We know this, too. And sometimes, following Jesus will lead us to the foot of a cross—where there is sorrow, yes, but even greater joy because of the hope we have in Him.

Many people find it difficult to accept this. They tell themselves, "Following Jesus should always lead to joy." But if you read about His disciples' fates in the New Testament, it's clear following Jesus is seldom the easy path to take in life.

As you move throughout the world, someone may dismiss you just for being a follower of Jesus Christ. You might lose out on a dating relationship you wanted but isn't spiritually good for you. You may be passed over for a promotion because you're not willing to play ball like everyone else at your workplace. There is hardship, but there is hope. It was true for Mary, and it's true for us: following Jesus doesn't mean everything in life is going to come easy, that every moment is going to be bursting with joy. There will be sorrowful times, too. But Jesus is with us, and He has already defeated what plagues us.

In John 16:33, Jesus says, "Here on earth you will have many trials and sorrows. But take heart, because I have overcome the world."

Discovery #3:
Following Jesus Is Filled With Miracle Moments.

What is a miracle moment? You can think of it as an event or experience that causes you to say, "Look at what God did." Big or small, it's not something you or someone else orchestrated, and it's more than coincidence. It's a moment in which God's hand was clearly involved. And we have moments like these every day, whether we take notice of them or not.

Maybe it's a marriage saved due to the prayers of the couple's new Bible study group at church. Perhaps it's a woman's years-long infertility struggle coming to an end when her and her husband's prayers are answered in the form of a pregnancy or a child to adopt. Miracle moments are those unexpected blessings when a door might close, but God opens another.

Think of how many miracle moments Mary had with Jesus during her life with Him.

One of the miracle moments Mary experienced with Jesus happened when He was 12. Mary and Joseph had just taken their family to Jerusalem for the Passover. They were traveling with hundreds of people, a crowd which included their family. As they were heading back home after the festival, they assumed Jesus was with the group. But when they looked, they couldn't find Him. It turns out they had left Jesus behind in Jerusalem.

If you're a parent, imagine the panic of having lost your child and not knowing where he or she is. Then think about if that child happened to be the Son of God that you were responsible for. In a panic, they went back to Jerusalem to look for Him.

Luke 2:46-51 continues the story:

"Three days later they finally discovered him in the Temple, sitting among the religious teachers, listening to them and asking questions. All who heard him were amazed at his understanding and his answers.

His parents didn't know what to think. 'Son,' his mother said to him, 'why have you done this to us? Your father and I have been frantic, searching for you everywhere.'

'But why did you need to search?' he asked. 'Didn't you know that I must be in my Father's house?' But they didn't understand what he meant.

Then he returned to Nazareth with them and was obedient to them. And his mother stored all these things in her heart."

In this story, Mary sees her 12-year-old boy schooling the community's religious leaders on what Scripture said. This is only one of many miracle moments Mary experienced with Jesus, but it's one she didn't simply forget. She didn't let the experience pass and move on. Luke 2:51 says she "stored all these things in her heart." She held on to that miracle moment with her Lord and Savior. And she stored it, like treasure, in her heart.

Every day, God is doing something only He can do. And like Mary, we need to hang on to those moments, those testimonies to God's glory, and store them in our hearts. Whether it's writing them down or sharing them with someone else, we shouldn't forget what God does for us—especially what His Son did at the cross. We know there will be tough times in life, moments filled with sorrow when all hope seems to be lost. But it's these miracle moments that strengthen our faith. It's these pockets of time—a rainbow darting through the sky after a powerful storm, a small kindness from a stranger when it's needed most—that remind us of the hope we have in God forever.

Discovery #4: Following Jesus Requires Faithfulness.

At one point in the New Testament, we read of a moment when Mary and Jesus' brothers tried to stop His ministry. We see that story in Mark 3. Jesus was teaching and healing people—in other words, turning Israel's spiritual and political world upside down—and His family thought He was out of His mind. They came to Him to take Him away from the ministry.

Mark 3:31 says:

"Then Jesus' mother and brothers came to see him. They stood outside and sent word for him to come out and talk with them. There was a crowd sitting around Jesus, and someone said, 'Your mother and your brothers are outside asking for you.'

Jesus replied, 'Who is my mother? Who are my brothers?'

Then he looked at those around him and said, 'Look, these are my mother and brothers. Anyone who does God's will is my brother and sister and mother.'"

Can you picture Mary waiting outside a crowded house, having summoned her son, who was also the Son of God, and this was

His response? That had to be painful for her to hear, but, at this moment, Mary needed to decide something important: Was she going to hold onto her role as Jesus' mother, or was she going to become a follower? Was she going to try to force her plan, or was she going to surrender her life and heart over to God entirely and follow His plan? The fact she followed Jesus to the cross reveals her answer.

==Faithfulness is making that initial decision to follow Jesus and then making a decision every day after that to surrender completely== and live your life for Him.

Now, that doesn't mean you have to pray to secure your salvation again with every new day. Once you've accepted Jesus in your heart, salvation is yours. It cannot be taken away. But every morning, you do have to recommit yourself to being a follower of Jesus. You have to recommit yourself to being faithful to Him, to surrendering to Him, to saying, "God, lead in every area of my life today. At work, in my relationships, at school, with my family, in everything I do, and with everyone I meet today, you take the lead. I surrender myself."

In Matthew 16:24, Jesus says, "If any of you wants to be my follower, you must give up your own way, take up your cross, and follow me."

It's not enough to surrender only the parts of your life that you want to. It's not enough to be faithful in some ways and unfaithful in others. Whether it's your relationships, job, finances, or daily habits—God wants you to surrender it all.

Think of it this way: Jesus surrendered Himself completely at the cross so we could have our sins forgiven. He died so the relationship between us and God that was broken by our sin could be restored. He gave His life so we could have a home in heaven. He sacrificed Himself so we could be the people God originally created us to be, to live the lives we are called to live. The one thing we needed most—salvation from our sins and a Savior to bring it about—God secured for us at the cross.

†

In Jesus' final moments on the cross, John 19:26-27 tells us Jesus saw His mother standing beside one of His disciples. In all His excruciating suffering, He noticed Mary in her sorrow.

And when Jesus saw her, John writes, "...he said to her, 'Dear woman, here is your son.' And he said to this disciple, 'Here is your mother.' And from then on this disciple took her into his home."

Mary's faithfulness was evident in her decision to follow Jesus to the cross, and even as He was dying, He comforted her, made a way for her, and, not to ruin the end of the story, came to her again after His resurrection. In other words, Jesus saw her faithfulness and rewarded her for it.

Hebrews 3:14 says, "For if we are faithful to the end, trusting God just as firmly as when we first believed, we will share in all that belongs to Christ."

AT THE CROSS

Thus might I hide my blushing face
While His dear cross appears.
Dissolve my heart in thankfulness,
And melt mine eyes to tears.

At the cross, at the cross where
I first saw the light,
And the burden of my heart rolled away,
It was there by faith I received my sight,
And now I am happy all the day!

"Alas, and Did My Savior Bleed"
Isaac Watts, *Hymns and Spiritual Songs* (1707)

4

AT THE CROSS WITH THE CONDEMNED CRIMINAL

*"Two others, both criminals,
were led out to be executed with him.
When they came to a place called
The Skull, they nailed him to the cross.
And the criminals were also crucified—
one on his right and one on his left."*
Luke 23:32-33

Let's return, one more time, to those final hours at the cross. Luke 23:32-35 portrays a devastating scene: two criminals were led out to be executed alongside Jesus, at the skull-shaped hill called Golgotha, one on His right, one on His left.

Awaiting death, one of the condemned beside the Son of God scoffed at Him, daring

Jesus to prove He was the Messiah. But the second criminal protested against the first, as Luke captures in Luke 23:40-41:

"Don't you fear God even when you have been sentenced to die? We deserve to die for our crimes, but this man hasn't done anything wrong."

If this criminal would've stopped there, one might think he believed Jesus was simply an innocent man wrongly convicted to death.

Except the criminal hanging beside Him said this next: "Jesus, remember me when you come into your Kingdom."

In the last moments of his life, this criminal believed Jesus was the Messiah, and he asked Jesus for salvation.

Luke 23:43 gives Jesus' reply:

"I assure you, today you will be with me in paradise."

Although we don't know everything about this condemned criminal, we do know that as he hung on the cross beside Jesus,

Jesus saw his fate after death. And despite everything he'd done in his life up to that point, this condemned criminal received God's salvation.

†

Key #1:
Salvation Is Offered By Grace.

On that tragic skull-shaped hill called Golgotha where thousands or more had been crucified, this criminal apprehended by the Roman government was fortunate enough in his hours of greatest despair to be divinely placed next to the Son of God, the Prince of Peace. Of all the days he could have been crucified, he was crucified at the same time as the Lord, the Savior of the world.

Historical records show crucifixion was a daily occurrence. The Romans crucified their enemies and convicted criminals in astounding numbers, hundreds and thousands at a time, to suppress and terrorize the people. There were far more men pacing Roman prisons about to be executed than those three hanging from the height of Golgotha that Friday afternoon. It could've been any one of them he hung beside, but instead, this condemned criminal had the profound blessing of meeting Jesus Christ, the Son of God, before he met his death.

And as if that wasn't blessing enough, Jesus said to him, "I assure you today you will be with me in paradise."

Now, why did Jesus say these words to this condemned criminal?

Because at the last possible moment, the criminal realized the sign posted above Jesus' head—"King of the Jews"—was true. Jesus was the promised Messiah, the true King of Israel.

Romans 5:7-8 says, "Now, most people would not be willing to die for an upright person, though someone might perhaps be willing to die for a person who is especially good. But God showed his great love for us by sending Christ to die for us while we were still sinners."

It didn't matter to Jesus that this criminal had made the kind of mistakes in life that ended with him on a cross. Jesus met him right where he was and promised him a fate he didn't deserve. But that's grace.

Grace means God offers us His salvation while we are still sinners. What does it mean to be saved? Salvation is God's process of forgiving our sins, of adopting us into His family, and securing our eternity forever in heaven through the death and resurrection of His Son, Jesus Christ.

When you believe in Jesus, it is a gift from God. Salvation is not a reward for the good things we have done, so none of us can boast about it. The condemned criminal teaches us, first, that God's salvation is by grace alone. It's nothing we do. This criminal had likely done little good in his life, but it didn't matter. Jesus was enough to forgive all his sins. If he did nothing else right, he believed in Jesus, and Jesus assured him of his salvation.

Key #2: Salvation Is Personal And Through Jesus Alone.

One of the ongoing misconceptions about God's offer of salvation is that it comes to people en masse. You may be from a mostly Christian country, such as Nigeria. But just because a lot of your friends or relatives have received salvation doesn't mean their salvation is also yours. If your parents are saved, that's great news, but you can't inherit their salvation because you're their child. Salvation comes to no one secondhand; it comes to people personally. You have the opportunity, right now, to end your rebellion against God and submit to Jesus Christ as your Lord and Savior. No one else can do that for you.

But how do you do it?

Romans 10:9 says, "If you openly declare that Jesus is Lord and believe in your heart that God raised him from the dead, you will be saved."

You see, salvation only comes through Jesus Christ. In fact, you can open your heart to Jesus right now by saying "Yes!" to Him as Savior and Lord of your life. In the next chapter, we'll walk you through exactly what this means, but you don't have to wait!

In Luke 23:43, it's Jesus, the Messiah, the Son of God, who tells the condemned criminal beside him what his fate is after death. The criminal asked Jesus for salvation, and Jesus gave it to him—through Himself.

You receive God's salvation through Jesus, or you don't receive it at all. That's why believers make such a big deal about Easter. The fact Jesus died on the cross and rose again three days later is the ultimate true story of hope for the world. God's one and only Son, Jesus, died for our sins and was raised again so we could be forgiven, so we could be close with God, so we could have new life in Jesus.

In John 14:6, the apostle John records Jesus' words: "I am the way, the truth, and the life. No one can come to the Father except through me."

Key #3: Salvation Is Immediate And For Eternity.

In Luke 23:43, we see the criminal's salvation happened in an instant. As soon as he believed in who Jesus was and what He was doing on the cross, Jesus assured him he would be with Him after death.

Like the condemned criminal, the moment you accept Jesus as your Lord and Savior, accept that what He endured on the cross covers all your sins, you will be saved. As Acts 2:21 says, "Everyone who calls on the name of the Lord will be saved."

If you've received God's salvation through Jesus Christ, you have it now and forever. There's no sin too bad or too burdensome to take away the hope God gives you in His Son when you believe in Him.

John 5:24 says as much: "I tell you the truth, those who listen to my message and believe in God who sent me have eternal life. They will never be condemned for their sins, but they have already passed from death into life."

Even the condemned criminal—condemned by the Roman government—would not be condemned by the real authority of heaven and earth—God—because he believed in Jesus. He believed Jesus was the Messiah.

As a result, Luke 23:43 tells us, "And Jesus replied, 'I assure you, today you will be with me in paradise.'"

First-century listeners, those who knew their Torah, the first five books of our Bible, would have immediately understood what that word, "paradise," signified. They would've known it pointed back to the very beginning of their story and sin's origin in the book of Genesis.

When God created Adam and Eve, He placed them in a perfect environment: the Garden of Eden, paradise. In Eden, there was no sin, no shame, no suffering. But through their pride in wanting to be like God and therefore disobeying the one command He gave them not to eat fruit from a specific tree, Adam and Eve lost paradise. However, beginning with the fall to sin in Genesis and throughout the Old Testament, God promised His people He would send a Messiah to offer salvation and restore the original paradise. A paradise lost would be a paradise found through this Savior.

For a criminal condemned to death on a cross, I'm sure the thought of that place called paradise, and the promise of getting to be there with Jesus, was the best hope his mind could've dwelt on as he took his final breath.

Imagine you were him—this condemned criminal. Do you know for sure if you were to die this very day that you would spend eternity with God in heaven? Do you know Jesus?

If you haven't decided to follow Jesus Christ, you're like the crucified criminal in many ways. Death is ruling over you. You're on your way to an eternity separated from God. But if you surrender your life to Jesus, if you believe in Him, in His death and resurrection three days later and the fact He paid the price for all your sins, you too can spend eternity with God in paradise—and live a changed life now here on earth.

The apostle Paul writes of this in Romans 5:17: "For the sin of this one man, Adam, caused death to rule over many. But even greater is God's wonderful grace and his gift of righteousness, for all who receive it will live in triumph over sin and death through this one man, Jesus Christ."

Maybe you know who Jesus is and where

you're spending your eternity, but who in your life doesn't?

Think about the eternity of your friends, your family, your neighbors, your coworkers, the people in your life who need God's salvation but who don't have a relationship with Him. It's not an accident God has put you in the lives of these individuals, just like it wasn't an accident the criminal on the cross was crucified by Jesus' side. God has placed you where you are intentionally. The people in your life desperately need to hear the story of the cross, the Gospel of Jesus Christ, so they too can receive salvation.

†

Remember the Savior of the world on that skull-shaped hill called Golgotha, where we picked up His story at the cross?

Can you see the sweat and the blood dripping down His cheeks as He turns to speak to the criminal beside Him, whose face is contorted with the pain of death? Do you hear Jesus' words to him—"I assure you, today you will be with me in paradise"—like balm on a searing wound?

Those are words everyone who has trusted Jesus as Savior should treasure in their heart if ever they lose hope, if ever they forget what happened at the cross, if ever it should slip their mind what occurred three days later—breath returned to a body, burial cloth in a heap on the ground of a tomb, a stone rolled away as the Son of God, the Messiah, conquered sin and death as the final act of God's grace...providing us with an eternal hope.

Hope for a hardened skeptic.

Hope for a devoted servant.

Hope for a heartbroken mother.

Hope for a condemned criminal.

Hope for you and me.

AT THE CROSS

But drops of grief can ne'er repay
The debt of love I owe;
Here, Lord, I give myself away,
'Tis all that I can do.

At the cross, at the cross where
I first saw the light,
And the burden of my heart rolled away,
It was there by faith I received my sight,
And now I am happy all the day!

"Alas, and Did My Savior Bleed"
Isaac Watts, *Hymns and Spiritual Songs* (1707)

YOU, AT THE CROSS

In the Bible, the apostle Paul describes what it means to have a saving encounter with Jesus: "If you openly declare that Jesus is Lord and believe in your heart that God raised him from the dead, you will be saved. For it is by believing in your heart that you are made right with God, and it is by openly declaring your faith that you are saved." (Romans 10:9-10)

Maybe you identify at times with our hardened skeptic, the Roman soldier who helped nail the Savior of the world to a cross—vengeful and hostile to God. You may see attributes in yourself similar to those of the devoted servant, Mary Magdalene, who had a life-altering encounter with the Messiah, and it changed her, humbled her, forever. Maybe you've been given an extraordinary task, a blessing with unique challenges, like our heartbroken mother, Mary.

Or perhaps it's the condemned criminal that seems most familiar to you, as you bear the painful consequences of your sin, but Jesus is meeting you there to offer grace. You likely see yourself in all four of these witnesses to the Crucifixion.

Regardless of your circumstance, no matter the brokenness you may feel from your sin or the damage sin has done to you and those you love, there is always hope in the Gospel.

At the cross, the Son of God assured that. His sacrificial death and resurrection three days later is the ultimate testimony of God's saving power, of His ability to transform darkness into light.

You never need to doubt Him.

Proverbs 3:5-6 says, "Trust in the Lord with all your heart; do not depend on your own understanding. Seek his will in all you do, and he will show you which path to take."

If this book is in your hands, but you have never asked Jesus into your life, take this moment, here and now, to pray this prayer:

Dear God, thank you for giving me the opportunity to know you. I open my heart to you and invite you into my life. I confess I am a sinner, and I ask you to forgive me of all my sins. I surrender all that I am to you and pray your will would be done in my life. From this moment on, I want to follow Jesus in the fellowship of His church. I believe you sent Him, your one and only Son, to die on a cross and rise again three days later, so that my sins would be forgiven and so that I could have an eternal home with you in Heaven. I trust Him alone as all I'll ever need to be able to stand in your holy presence. I'm in your hands. Help me to walk with you. In Jesus' name, I pray. Amen.

Even though you may not understand all that it means right now, if you've prayed this prayer and believe in your heart that these words are true, you now have the hope of a new, better future in Jesus. Be sure to tell your pastor about the decision you've made, and know that God is with you as you start this incredible journey surrendering your life…at the cross.

ACKNOWLEDGMENTS

Nelson Searcy: I would first like to express my eternal thanks to Jesus Christ, God's Son, and what he did for me "at the cross" 2,000 years ago. I have had the privilege of following Jesus (imperfectly) since my freshman year in college. Thank you, God!

For this book, I must express my appreciation to C. A. Meyer, a former member and group leader at The Journey Church, who moved away to pursue seminary, teaching and writing. This is the first book we have co-authored together. Her gifts of unique phrasing and creative writing plus a deep and positive commitment to Scripture have made this unlike any other book I've ever written. While my gifts are more on the "logic side," her gifts are more on the "creative side" and this made for a great writing partnership.

It's no understatement to say that this book would not be in your hands without the exceptional management and guidance of Sandra Olivieri, Vice President at Church Leader Insights. Her gentle hand guided this project from start to finish. Using her management, creative and journalism skills, she made the content of the book stronger and the physical/e-book a reality. Thank you, Sandra.

Many others contributed to this book as well. While the idea of "At the Cross" was mine, it was originally the teaching team at The Journey Church who helped me bring the ideas alive, led by my long-time colleagues Pastor Kerrick Thomas and Pastor Jason Hatley—who both continually push themselves to deeper engagement with Scripture, inspirational communication and personal growth. Pastor Jeremy Brock, a member of our Teaching Team at the time, particularly contributed to the chapter on Mary Magdalene, challenging us to go deeper into her history.

ACKNOWLEDGMENTS

A special thank you to Matthew C. Easter, PhD—also a former member of the Journey Teaching Team but currently a Professor at Missouri Baptist University—who offered theological insight. To Richard Jarman, my co-author on other books, Sandra Olivieri and Kerrick Thomas who all offered insights and editorial suggestions. The book is stronger for their comments but the errors, theologically and grammatically, are mine alone.

Finally, my writing ministry—which now stretches to approximately 20 books—would not be possible without the commitment of my family. I write during discretionary times as my primary ministry is The Journey Church, so my wife, Kelley, and son, Alexander, have to deal with my early morning writing habits, odd hours locked away in my home office and occasional requests for just a few more minutes "while I wrap up this section." While writing this book my wife and I celebrated our 26th wedding anniversary by eating at home during the Coronavirus lockdown. But my son continued his Karate lessons via Zoom and social distancing and earned his black belt. Bruh! I am blessed beyond measure.

C.A. Meyer: Thank you to the Father, Son, and Spirit for inspiring and guiding this remembrance of Jesus' sacrifice at the cross. I pray this work and its reception is all for Your glory. Thank you to Nelson, Sandra, and the entire Church Leader Insights team for inviting me to work alongside you and patiently mentoring me throughout the process with equal parts professionalism and friendship. Thank you to Stephen Curto for your generosity, wise counsel, and faith-filled support throughout this endeavor. Lastly, I thank God for DTS-Houston, the First Pres Kingwood community, my loving friends, and, of course, my incredible family. What a tremendous blessing to get to do life with you this side of heaven.

BOOKS BY NELSON SEARCY

Brand New!
The Generosity Secret: How to Get Out of Debt and Find Financial Freedom
Topic: Personal Finance

Best Seller!
The New You: A Guide to Better Physical, Mental, Emotional, and Spiritual Wellness
Topic: Health, Spiritual Growth

The Renegade Pastor's Guide to Managing the Stress of Ministry
Topic: Leadership

The Renegade Pastor's Guide to Time Management
Topic: Leadership

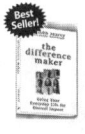

Best Seller!
The Difference Maker: Using Your Everyday Life for Eternal Impact
Topic: Evangelism, Spiritual Growth

The Greatness Principle: Finding Significance and Joy by Serving Others
Topic: Recruiting Volunteers

Top Seller!
The Generosity Ladder: Your Next Step to Financial Peace
Topic: Stewardship

Revolve: A New Way To See Worship
Topic: Worship

The Renegade Pastor: Abandoning Average in Your Life and Ministry
Topic: Leadership

Best Seller!
Fusion: Turning First-Time Guests Into Fully Engaged Members of Your Church
Topic: Assimilation

These books are available at Amazon.com and ChristianBook.com
For other resources, visit www.ChurchLeaderInsights.com

HOW TO BREAK FREE FROM FINANCIAL STRESS

The Generosity Secret: How to Get Out of Debt and Find Financial Freedom

Nelson Searcy and Jennifer Dykes Henson provide a systematic approach to handling money in a God-honoring way that guides you step-by-step away from a life of financial strain to a new reality of financial health and freedom!

Readers will discover how to:

- get out of debt — and stay out
- set smart goals for spending, saving, and giving
- live and give in a fulfilling way
- and much more

Anyone who is ready to stop stressing about money will find *The Generosity Secret* to be an effective guide for living and giving in a fulfilling, God-honoring way.

Available at at these book retailers and more:

amazon

BARNES&NOBLE

Christianbook.com

BAKER BOOK HOUSE

HOW TO USE YOUR LIFE TO MAKE A DIFFERENCE

The Difference Maker: Using Your Everyday Life for Eternal Impact

God has uniquely positioned you to influence those around you for him. He wants to partner with you in changing people's lives both now — and for eternity.

This practical guide from Nelson Searcy, with Jennifer Dykes Henson, will show you how you can begin using your everyday life to make a difference in the lives of those who don't know Jesus.

Through this powerful book, you will:

- Know the power of your personal story and how God can use it to transform others

- Be ready to be used by God, no matter where you are

- Avoid feeling intimidated in talking about your faith

Are you ready to be a Difference Maker?

Available at:
amazon   **BARNES&NOBLE**

To order in bulk, visit www.ChurchLeaderInsights.com

HOW TO IMPROVE YOUR HEALTH IN 4 KEY AREAS

The New You: A Guide to Better Physical, Mental, Emotional and Spiritual Wellness

How many of us are living up to our full, God-given potential? What's holding us back — and how can we overcome it?

These are the questions Nelson Searcy and Jennifer Dykes Henson want us to ask — and answer — with the help of *The New You*.

Readers come away with specific strategies to:

- lose weight
- get more sleep
- lower stress
- nurture better relationships
- connect with God
- and much more

Anyone who wants to trade in the frustration of average living and less-than health for the hallmarks of the new life God promises will find *The New You* an effective personal guide for the journey.

Available at at these book retailers and more:

amazon

BARNES & NOBLE

Christianbook.com

BAKER BOOK HOUSE